Biblical MEDITATION

The Secret to a Transformed Life

Study Guide

CARLTON BABATUNDE WILLIAMS

www.soundink.com

Cover Design and Layout by Dare Emmanuel of Sound Ink Media (media@sound-ink.com).

Acknowledgements

I will always be grateful to Dr. Peter Ilori, whose insight into the scriptures challenged me many years ago, thrusting me on a path to deeper study and hunger for intimacy with God. My pastor, Bob Yandian, has set for me a standard of integrity and doctrinal soundness to which I aspire. I would also like to acknowledge and thank my mentor, Geof Jackson, for putting up with my incessant questioning and spiritual naiveté during my time at Grace Bible School and loving me through it all.

There are people God sends into your life that are important to your journey. I believe my editors, Timi Yeseibo, Kemi Odukoya and designer Dare Emmanuel are such people. Thank you for the tireless hours spent on revisions, editing, and painstaking re-designs that helped arrive at this final product.

I thank God for you all.

How To Use The Study Guide

Meditation holds the key to unlocking the transforming power of God in every life, and it has the potential to ignite revival fire in every heart. The way the word meditation is used today deviates from the original meaning in the Hebrew and Greek texts of the Bible, dampening its effectiveness. However, biblical meditation started with the patriarchs and persisted throughout the early church. God told Joshua that meditation is the recipe for a prosperous journey in life (Joshua 1:8).

This study guide is designed as an accompaniment to the book, Biblical Meditation. It will enable you to hone your understanding of the concepts shared in Biblical Meditation by exploring questions, which expose any underlying beliefs, for further reflection and discussion. It will also challenge you to examine the practical ways these concepts can be applied and lived out.

While the study guide is intended for group settings whether small or large, facilitated by leaders who have read Biblical Meditation, it can also be used for personal study. I recommend that readers begin by first completing Biblical Meditation, to receive a holistic understanding of the subject of meditation. Then start again, reading a chapter of the book before delving into the corresponding chapter in the study guide. The chapters in the study guide match the chapters in the book. It is best to take a sequential approach, building understanding and steering discussions from the first chapter to the last.

Only some of the scripture passages referred to are written out in the study guide, so it is good to have a Bible with you as you go through the book. Writing space is provided to record your answers and reflections. Feel free however, to use a journal or other writing material to capture thoughts and information that do not fit in the space provided.

Start each session with prayer, asking the Holy Spirit to give you insight. Inspired

Bible prayers can be found in the appendices. Essential study aids for your devotional life are also listed. Many are my personal favourites.

Work through the study guide at a comfortable pace for you or for your group. The goal of meditation is not to finish but to be transformed. It is my prayer that as you journey through the study guide, you will receive insight into this ancient path and claim meditation back with its true meaning and practice.

I commend this book to the precious Body of Christ who have been purchased by the blood of the Lamb of God and called to a high purpose. May your heart's hunger for more of God be satisfied through the power of the Holy Spirit.

Table of Contents

Introduction

In today's world, meditation is a word that is widely used among people who consider themselves somewhat spiritual or religious. Some Christians view the word with suspicion, falling for the enemy's classic manoeuvre: make people let go of a powerful truth by calling a falsehood the same name.

▶   We think in pictures. When you read the word, dog, you don't see the letters d-o-g. You see a dog in your mind's eye. When you hear the word meditation, what picture comes to mind?

____

____

____

▶   Did you see a Buddhist statue with the signature crossed legs, a woman wearing yoga pants in a classic yoga pose, or a man on a mat holding prayer beads and muttering? Explain why a particular picture comes to your mind when you hear the word meditation.

____

____

____

____

____

▶ How have the images you have of meditation affected our attitude towards the practice?

____

____

____

____

▶ Think of other words whose meaning or connotation have changed over time. What about words from the Bible that have lost their original meaning over time? Why is this so?

____

____

____

____

Christians today have more access to the Bible and study materials than at any other period in church history and the majority in the West enjoy religious freedom. However, we do not readily see the powerful witness described in the book of Acts or the same potency of the first century 120 who transformed their world.

The word of God remains the same and the Holy Spirit remains on earth. We are still in the same dispensation as that of the church in the book of Acts. What did they know and understand that we need to learn?

▶ Would you agree that Christians today have greater access to the Bible, books, and study materials than ever before? Are we having the same results and widespread influence as the early church? Give reasons for your answer.

____

____

____

____

____

____

▶ How can the church have greater relevance in society? What Christian practices should undergird what the church is doing?

____

____

____

____

____

Part One

The Case For Meditation

Chapter 1

The Fruitful Life

Read Psalm One.

Blessed is the man
Who walks not in the counsel of the ungodly,
Nor stands in the path of sinners,
Nor sits in the seat of the scornful;
But his delight is in the law of the LORD,
And in His law he meditates day and night.
He shall be like a tree
Planted by the rivers of water,
That brings forth its fruit in its season,
Whose leaf also shall not wither;
And whatever he does shall prosper.
The ungodly are not so,
But are like the chaff which the wind drives away.
Therefore the ungodly shall not stand in the judgment,
Nor sinners in the congregation of the righteous.
For the LORD knows the way of the righteous,
But the way of the ungodly shall perish (Psalm 1:1-6).

▶ **What are the elements of a fruitful life?**

WALKING, STANDING, SITTING

Momentum does not indicate success. It is not the fact that you are moving that matters. Have you ever watched a tree falling? You can almost tell the exact spot where it will end up. It starts with motion, gains momentum, but ends up stationary. Using the tree analogy, the direction where you are falling is what makes the difference. Any lumberjack will tell you that when felling trees, the direction of the wind does not determine where the tree falls. The lumberjack determines the direction of the fall by the angle of his cut. Before a seed breaks through the ground and pushes its stem upwards, a root system must have first developed beneath, where no one can see. In the same way, a failed life does not just happen.

▶ **Describe the progression on the path to failure described in Psalm One.**

" *If you have succumbed to counsel, that set you in the direction of failure, change your course by delighting in God's word and meditating on it.* **"**

▶ Have you ever received counsel from someone you respect that didn't sit right with you? Describe the internal conflict that resulted from that and how you resolved it.

____

____

____

____

____

▶ Review the last three important decisions you made and examine your sources of counsel. With what you have learnt so far how would you have approached the process differently?

____

____

____

____

____

▶ Be honest about what is driving you. What is the motivation behind your momentum? What gets you out of bed every morning? Give a one word answer.

____

____

If you have succumbed to counsel, which has set you in the direction of failure, you can change your course. Your negative prevailing circumstances do not have to determine the outcome of your life, you can still take control. Success is not just about what we don't do, it is also about the right actions we take.

▶ What action(s) can you take that will place you on the road to success?

____

____

____

____

____

____

VALUE + PURSUIT = PLEASURE + DELIGHT

Delight can be defined as extreme pleasure. The prosperous man finds his joy and pleasure in God's word. Pleasure is dictated by the direction of one's heart or passion.

▶ Consider the meaning of delight. Are you delighted to study God's word?

____

____

▶ Is it possible to increase the joy and pleasure you derive from God's word and if so, how can this be done?

____

____

____

____

____

____

UNMOVED BY HEAT AND DROUGHT

❝ *The firm roots that provide stability in times of pressure only develop when meditation is a habitual practice.* **❞**

If you fall to pieces in a crisis, there wasn't much to you in the first place (Proverbs 24:10 The Message).

▶ How can meditation prepare us to meet the challenges that pressure brings?

____

____

____

____

____

____

OUTCOMES WITHIN OUR REACH

God does not determine our success or failure in life. Success and failure are outcomes that are determined by actions that are within our control. The only reference to God in Psalm One is found in the last verse. There is a path of righteousness already marked out and anyone who walks that path will prosper. The path we choose to take is up to us, it is not pre-determined.

▶   Read Deuteronomy 30:19. What role does God play in the choices we make?

____

____

____

____

____

____

▶   What is the single most important choice we must make to have a fruitful outcome in our lives?

____

Chapter 2

The Bread of Life

I believe it is significant that Jesus compared the word of God to bread. Just as physical bread gives life to the body, the word of God is spiritual bread that nourishes the spiritual part of man.

But He answered and said, "It is written: 'Man shall not live by bread alone, but by every word that proceeds from the mouth of God,'" (Matthew 4:4).

▶ Discuss the similarities between bread and the word of God.

PHYSICAL VERSUS SPIRITUAL SUBSTANCE

LIFE SOURCE

FRESH

AVAILABILITY

NEED FOR PREPARATION

FOR CONSUMPTION

DIGESTION

ENERGY COMES AFTER FOOD HAS BEEN DIGESTED

Meditation is the process by which the spirit of man gets his nourishment. The word of God can be admired, treasured, applauded, and even agreed with, but until it is consumed and digested, it will be of no benefit to our spiritual man.

" The word of God contains the nutrients that our spiritual man requires for a healthy and satisfying existence. "

Can you imagine what life would be like if you had no energy? We expend energy in every activity even if it is a small amount. If you were to go into a gym right now, I am sure there are certain weights that you would not be able to lift. You may go in with all the determination and positivity you can muster, but your ability to lift weights depends on your strength level. With a disciplined training programme, your strength level will gradually increase, and you will be able to lift heavier and heavier weights.

We need to look at the word of God in exactly the same way. If it is like bread, and if digesting the word produces spiritual energy, then there are certain desires, which we will not be able to lay hold of right now, because we have not developed the spiritual strength to receive them. We receive and experience everything God has given us in Christ and all that He plans for our lives through faith. Faith is a tangible spiritual substance produced by consuming and digesting God's word.

▶ Describe a time when you were frustrated spiritually because you were yet to receive something you prayed for.

▶ In retrospect, was the frustration because you had not yet developed the spiritual strength to receive your desires? Give reasons for your answer.

According to Jamieson's Commentary on the Old and New Testament, "Meditation upon, is to reading the Word what digesting is to eating. Without the slow and lengthened process of digestion, food would not nourish the body; without meditation, the Word read, will not nourish the soul."[1]

GROWTH IS A PROCESS

We grow and develop in faith and in grace. We need to start with the little things and gradually build up to the next level.

▶ From what you have learnt so far, what is spiritual energy and how is it produced?

---

1 Robert Jamieson, A.R. Fausset, and David Brown, A Commentary On The Old And New Testament, Volume 2 (Massachusetts: Hendrickson, 1997), 105.

▶ Where can you apply spiritual energy right now to begin to see results in your life?

Chapter 3

The Digested Word

The word of God has inherent creative power to produce what it proclaims.

So shall My word be that goes forth from My mouth; It shall not return to Me void, but it shall accomplish what I please, and prosper in the thing for which I sent it (Isaiah 55:11).

For no word of God shall be void of power (Luke 1:37 ASV).

WHAT ARE YOU ATTENDING TO?

The word of God operates like medicine. When a capsule is swallowed, somewhere in your stomach, the sheath that houses the medicine breaks open and the medicine is absorbed into your body to effect the cure. To be effective, you must take the medicine according to the prescribed dosage. The passage below gives us the recommended dosage of God's word that will get the results it guarantees.

My son, give attention to my words; incline your ear to my sayings. Do not let them depart from your eyes; Keep them in the midst of your heart; For they are life to those who find them, and health to all their flesh (Proverbs

4:20-22).

▶   What kind of focus on God's word is required from us?

____

____

____

▶   What are the top factors that distract us from the required focus we should give to God's word?

____

____

____

____

▶   What strategies can we employ to achieve the level of focus recommended?

____

____

____

____

____

▶ When our hearts are filled with doubt and fear, what is this an indication of?

____

____

____

STRENGTH TO LIVE RIGHT

> **"** *God's word is of no use to us on a page. It must be digested and absorbed into our being through meditation to produce spiritual energy.* **"**

Many Christians are beaten over the head with messages about the importance of living right. They are implored, challenged, and even threatened to live by the high moral standards and integrity that the word of God commands. However, character is not developed because you tell people to develop character. The stranglehold of habits that keep people bound is not going to be broken because you say, "Just do it!" Most people want to be of good character and possess healthy habits, but they find themselves too weak to fight negative cycles of behaviour and evil compulsions.

You can't bench-press one hundred kilograms just because you are told to do so or desire to do so. To succeed, you have to develop the strength required to push off that weight. It doesn't matter how many times people shout at you or encourage you, unless they furnish you with the tools you need to develop the strength to bench-press that weight, they are not contributing to your success.

This book of the Law shall not depart from your mouth, but you shall meditate in it day and night, that you may observe to do according to all that is written in it. For then you will make your way prosperous, and then you will have good success (Joshua 1:8).

God was not saying that Joshua should meditate on the word so that when he came against opposition he would merely remember what His word said. No, it goes beyond that. When you meditate on the word, you are consuming the word, which is similar to eating bread and receiving the physical energy needed to work because the bread has been digested and nutrients absorbed. When you meditate on God's word, you receive spiritual energy from the word that enables you obey the word.

▶ **What is the role of willpower in developing character?**

▶ **Where does the strength to live right come from?**

TRUTH BRINGS FREEDOM

It takes the operation of the power of God to set people free from bad habits, demonic oppression, and sickness. Jesus said that if you know the truth, the power of that truth would make you free. God hasn't called us to set ourselves free. The power that brings freedom is in His word.

▶ **Read John 8:31-32. How can we know the truth that brings freedom?**

____

____

____

____

____

____

____

▶ **How often does the Bible recommend that we meditate on the word to achieve success in our lives?**

____

FAITH COMES, FAITH GOES

God's word is His agent for effectiveness. This is the process. God gives us His word which contains the supernatural energy for its fulfillment. We receive the word into our hearts and consume it through meditation. Then we are filled with the same energy the word contains. As we walk in His energy, doing what He has commanded in His strength, we receive the result He promised.

▶ Who is the active agent in our prosperity? Give the scriptural reference that supports your assertion.

____

____

____

____

Faith comes by hearing and hearing by the word of God (Romans 10:17).

According to Romans 10:17, faith comes. This means it is not always there. Energy is tangible. Every physical activity expends your energy and after a while, you need to replenish your energy supply otherwise your body will give way. Spiritual energy operates the same way; you build it up and expend it.

> **❝** *Meditating on God's word produces spiritual energy that enables you to obey the word.* **❞**

What we do with the word determines how much spiritual energy we produce. Faith does not come because you heard something several years ago; it comes by hearing.

▶ When you are low on physical energy, how do you behave?

____

____

____

▶ Can you tell when your spiritual energy is low?

____

____

____

▶ What yardstick do you use to measure your spiritual energy level?

____

____

____

▶ What can you do to remedy the situation if you are low on spiritual energy?

____

____

____

▶ To be effective in our daily lives, how do we maintain our spiritual energy levels?

____

____

____

Chapter 4

More Than Physical

But He answered and said, "It is written, 'Man shall not live by bread alone, but by every word that proceeds from the mouth of God,'" (Matthew 4:4).

Jesus did not say, "Man shall not live by bread," but "Man shall not live by bread alone," signifying that there is much more to mankind than what physical nourishment can satisfy. There is a dimension to human life that can only be satisfied by every word that comes from the mouth of God.

IN THE IMAGE OF GOD

Did You not . . .
Clothe me with skin and flesh,
And knit me together with bones and sinews? (Job 10:10–11).

The word 'me' in the verses above, does not refer to Job's body because he refers to his skin and flesh as his clothes. Paul sheds more light on this.

Now may the God of peace Himself sanctify you completely; and may your whole spirit, soul, and body be preserved blameless at the coming of our Lord Jesus Christ (1 Thessalonians 5:23).

According to 1 Thessalonians 5:23, man is a tripartite being. He is spirit, soul, and body. Each part of man is important because Paul prayed for the preservation of every part until the coming of the Lord.

▶ According to Genesis 1:27 and John 4:24 who are you?

____

____

▶ What are some characteristics of spirits?

____

____

____

____

____

▶ What implications does knowing you are spirit have for you?

____

____

____

____

THE MIND OF MAN & THE HUMAN SYSTEM

After the new birth, the Lord who is Spirit, lives in our spirits in the person of the Holy Spirit (1 Corinthians 6:19). The spirit is the inner or inward man referred to in Ephesians 3:16 and 2 Corinthians 4:16. The Holy Spirit knows everything that

God has planned for you and resides within your spirit to share these secrets with you (1 Corinthians 2:12). Your inward knower, also called intuition, is really the witness of the Holy Spirit with your spirit concerning truth. It can be described as a red or green light from your spirit and is a safe guide regarding all maters (1 John 5:10).

The soul consists of the mind, will, and emotions. The conscious mind consists of the intellect, memory, and imagination, but there is also a more powerful hidden subconscious mind, which is where our belief systems, lusts (evil desires), and conscience reside. The soul receives input from the spiritual, mental, and physical realms and is the avenue through which we express ourselves physically or spiritually. Though the soul can express both physical and spiritual things, the soul is a spiritual entity.

Your brain is not your soul. Your brain is where your soul resides for as long as you dwell in your physical body, and it is the physical conduit by which commands are sent from your soul for physical expression. When you leave this earth, your soul leaves with you. If a man suffers brain damage or some sort of brain degenerative disease, he may lose the ability to express his soul through his physical body. Though his brain is damaged, his soul remains intact.

In the story of the rich man and Lazarus (Luke 16: 19-31), when the rich man died and went to hell, he recognized Lazarus and remembered his father's house, his five brothers, and the cooling effect of water. His soul was intact, showing that the soul, though housed in the brain while we are in the body, is however a spiritual part of man.

▶   Read 1 Corinthians 6:19 and John 14:16-17. Where does the Holy Spirit reside?

▶ According to 1 Corinthians 2:12, what role does the Holy Spirit play within us? Give an example of how you have experienced Him carry out His role within you.

____

____

____

▶ At the point of death, which part(s) of man will remain on earth and which part(s) will go to Heaven/Hell?

____

____

> **"** *The conscience is a safe guide when it is enlightened by the truth of God's word.* **"**

The primary arena Satan and his forces attack in a human being is the soul. His aim is to establish a stronghold of belief systems that are contrary to God's truth in the subconscious mind. Through deceit, Satan uses a person's imagination, memory, fleshly impulses, and intellect, to build contrary belief systems and evil desires in their subconscious. If left unchallenged, he will successfully dull their sensitivity to right and wrong by increasingly building a resistance to and ultimately searing their conscience through repeated wilful disobedience.

Your spirit expresses itself in your subconscious (soul), through your conscience. The conscience is a safe guide when it is enlightened by the truth of God's word. The emotions, siding with the subconscious mind will always empower the will to act out what is established in the subconscious mind even when it is contrary to what one would consciously like to do.

▶ **Where is the seat of our belief systems?**

When the Bible speaks about the heart of man, it is referring to the spiritual core of the human system, which is the place of union of the spirit and the subconscious mind. Whoever controls the subconscious mind of a human being controls the actions of that life. The power of the Holy Spirit working through meditation uproots established satanic belief systems in our subconscious mind and replaces them with the truth of God.

> **“** *Sustained meditation is important to establish God's word in our hearts, which is where real transformation occurs.* **”**

Real transformation only occurs in the heart. If the impact of the word of God is limited to the memory (we can recite it), or intellect (we agree with it), during times of pressure, we will always default to what is established in our subconscious. This is why sustained mediation is important. The truth of God's word must be established in our hearts before it will affect our actions.

▶ **What drives a human being's actions? Explore the differences between the conscious and sub-conscious mind and give examples of how you have experienced the functioning of both.**

▶   Given what you have learnt about the soul, why is your soul
important?

____

____

____

____

____

▶   Read Proverbs 23:7, Matthew 12:35, and Psalm 119:11. Where does
real transformation begin? What are the elements for transformation?

____

____

____

____

____

____

With our bodies, we contact the physical world and provide input to our souls.
The body is a tent (2 Corinthians 5:1), a home for our spirits to reside while on earth.

*For as the body without the spirit is dead, so faith without works is dead
also (James 2:26).*

The spirit does not need the body to live, but the body needs the spirit to remain alive. Discarding a shirt you have worn all day does not in any way affect or damage your body. In the same way, when your body is discarded at the time of physical death, you (i.e. your spirit and soul) are not damaged in any way.

▶ Why is your body important?

How much care and attention should you devote to your body?

▶ Discuss: the expressions and actions of your body are a reflection of the state of your soul.

MORE THAN THE PHYSICAL

For generations man has searched for meaning. There is a deep yearning in humanity for more. Achievement and success haven't satisfied this hunger. Sexual immorality has failed dismally in delivering on its promise of freedom and has only led to more bondage and despair. Drugs have not satisfied.

> **"** *There is a deeper dimension to human life that can only be satisfied by every word that comes from the mouth of God.* **"**

Man's spirit and soul yearn for that which can satisfy. Physical substances can never satisfy spiritual hunger. The only substance that can satisfy the hunger of man's heart is the word of God.

▶ When people speak about an emptiness on the inside and allude to a search for significance, what is really happening to them?

____

____

____

____

▶ Have you ever felt that way? What can you do about it? What practical measures can you take?

____

____

____

Part **Two**
The Art of Meditation

Chapter 5

The Art of Meditation

MEDITATE IS A VERB

The word translated 'meditate' is the Hebrew word *hâgâh*, which denotes an active recitation[2] and means to carefully reflect on the matter in hand and to mutter.[3] *Hâgâh* in Hebrew thought and practice is different from the English meditation, which is a quiet reflection and is purely a mental exercise. In Hebrew practice, meditation fluctuates between thinking and speaking. To meditate on the scriptures is to repeat them quietly in a soft monotonous sound, while utterly abandoning outside distractions. It is a dynamic action, not a passive one.

> **❝** *Meditation is a vocal and mental process that involves weighing, pondering, revolving in the mind, and muttering.* **❞**

In the New Testament, the word 'meditate' is translated from the Greek word *meletaō*, which takes the same meaning as its Hebrew counterpart in the active

---

2   Notes from Joshua 1:8, *New Spirit Filled Life Bible*, (Nashville: Thomas Nelson, 2002), 279.

3   James H. Strong, *Strong's Exhaustive Concordance* (Michigan: Baker Book House, 1989), H1897

involvement of speech, attention, and imagination. [4]   It is a vocal and mental process that involves weighing, pondering, revolving in the mind, and muttering. For example, an orator would review a speech in his mind or practise a speech before addressing an audience. These are not passive actions. An actor for instance visualizes himself as the character, becomes one with the part, and goes on stage to play who he has become.

▶   **Is the explanation given for meditation similar or different from any other you might have heard? How is it similar or different?**

____

____

____

____

____

MUTTER, CONTEMPLATE, VISUALIZE, MUTTER

Have you ever taken note of the preparation routine of athletes before an event? I've noticed this particularly with triple jumpers.

They stand at the starter's mark and look ahead of them, down the path to the pit. You can watch them rehearse how they plan to make the jump. Sometimes they can be heard muttering phrases like, "you can do it, you can do it," as they look towards the finish line.

---

4   *The Complete Biblical Library, Greek-English Dictionary Lamda-Omicron*, (Missouri: World Library Press, 1990), 142.

Meditating on God's word works in a similar way. You mutter to yourself and visualize yourself in the word. You see yourself as who God says you are in the scriptures. You see yourself in present possession of what the scriptures say you have.

► **From the examples given about the orator and the athlete, what are some of the elements of meditation?**

____

____

____

► **Have you ever meditated on something other than God's word? Give examples.**

____

____

____

GETTING STARTED

You begin meditation by approaching the verse with the attitude that God is speaking to you. You focus on a verse or a few verses of scripture. You can't meditate on a book of the Bible. You can't even meditate on a chapter of the Bible. Next, receive that verse into your mind with the aim of focusing on it. You do not need to consciously memorize a verse of scripture to meditate on it. In meditation, your spiritual man is consuming the word just as your body consumes food. Once the verse is consumed, it will become a part of you, and you can reproduce it as if you had memorized it. The difference is that a scripture meditated on does not just remain in your mind; it resides in your heart.

It is the Spirit who gives life; the flesh profits nothing. The words that I speak to you are spirit, and they are life (John 6:63).

" *The word of God in your mind will not change your life, but the word of God in your heart will transform you.* "

The words Jesus spoke were not aimed at the natural man but at the spiritual part of man. When received into the heart, His words produce spiritual energy and strength in the part of man that affects his whole life.

► **Why isn't it possible to meditate on a book or chapter of the Bible?**

____

____

____

____

► **What is the difference between biblical meditation and scripture memorization?**

____

____

____

____

____

After reading the verse you want to meditate on, close your eyes and repeat (mutter) as many words of the verse as you can remember aloud. Open your eyes and read the parts of the verse you couldn't remember. Repeat this process until the verse is received into your mind. Continue by muttering the words to yourself, focusing on each word and making it personal.

MAKING SENSE OF WORDS

You cannot meditate on a verse if there are words in the verse you don't understand. How can you absorb the nutrients in food if it hasn't been properly broken down? The verse must be properly broken down or understood before it can be absorbed.

One of the questions we ask during meditation is this: what did the words used by the writer mean in his day? Looking up a word in the English dictionary will only tell you how the word is used today not how it was used when your Bible version was translated. For a dictionary to be useful in understanding the wording in the King James Version of the Bible for instance, it would have to be a dictionary written in the seventeenth century when the King James Version was translated.

Reading from a modern translation of the Bible helps, although it is not foolproof because the English language is in a process of constant change. The best solution is to use study aids that give the meaning of the words in the original languages, Hebrew for Old Testament verses, and Koine Greek for New Testament verses.

▶ Why is it important to understand the words in the verse(s) of scripture you are meditating on?

▶   To be effective, what aids do you need during your time of meditation?

____

____

____

BEYOND MENTAL ASSENT

During meditation, we focus, mutter, and use our imagination to place ourselves in the verse, chewing on it, and making it ours. But, what about your weaknesses and the sin you committed last week? Do you hear that familiar condemning thought rise up in your mind as you meditate?

While meditating, the word of God begins to paint a true picture of who you are and what you have, in your heart. That picture may be at odds with your experience. However, you have to look your weaknesses or your circumstances in the eye and continue to declare what the verse of scripture says about you and your situation.

> **"***During meditation, a new picture of who you are and what you have is painted in your heart.***"**

As you continue to focus on what God says about you and mutter it to yourself, something begins to happen inside you. Your identity changes because a new understanding about your true nature and character dawns on you and with that understanding comes energy. That energy is called faith. It is the spiritual strength needed to walk in who the word says you are; the strength to walk like the child of God you are.

▶ What kinds of *distractions* can show up during meditation?

____

____

____

____

____

❝*During meditation, you see yourself as who God says you are and in present possession of what the scriptures say you have.***❞**

▶ How can we overcome them?

____

____

____

____

____

In the process of meditation, the word and I become one. It is neither hypocrisy nor a mind game. I take on the personality of the word. This is how we walk in every aspect of scripture. Whether it is your covenant with God, who you are in Christ, or living a holy life, the power to walk in God's word is released through meditation.

▶ In which aspect of your life do you need the greatest transformation?

____

____

____

▶ What verse(s) of scripture can you start meditating on to activate change?

____

____

____

____

____

____

Chapter 6

The Practice of Meditation

Bread is prepared from flour, yeast, water, and salt. Depending on the tenderness, flavour, and colour desired, oils, shortening, butter, and eggs might also be added. These ingredients need to be measured out, mixed in the right quantity and order, and then baked in the oven for a certain length of time.

THE NEED FOR PREPARATION & PREPARING YOUR MEAL

Wouldn't you consider it strange if somebody told you, "Why bother following the bread recipe, you know what the ingredients are don't you? Just drink one and a quarter cups of water, swallow a teaspoon of salt and yeast, and three cups of flour, and you'll be fine!" Ingesting the ingredients will not have the same effect as eating the finished product. If you were to follow this misguided advice, you would most certainly fall ill.

In the same way, the word of God needs to be prepared from the scriptures. The scriptures in turn need to be studied and arranged in a certain format before being ingested.

▶ Why isn't it advisable to pull out a verse of scripture randomly to meditate on?

____

____

____

____

HOW SHOULD WE STUDY THE BIBLE?

There are several methods of studying the Bible. All the different methods are beneficial and should be practised.

> **"** *We have already gained God's approval through our faith in Christ. Through study, we demonstrate our approval.* **"**

One method is reading the Bible from cover to cover, from Genesis to Revelation. This gives the reader an overview of how God has dealt with humanity through the ages and a balanced view of the spirit of God's word.

Another method is to carry out a book study, where you establish the background of the book, why the letter was written to this church or person, when it was written, and what key problems the writer was trying to address. Knowledge about the book's setting helps us to interpret the verses in the light of what was happening at the time and helps to clear up difficulties that we may encounter as we try to understand the book.

Sometimes we are drawn to study a particular verse of scripture that is relevant to something we may be going through at the time. This is called an exegetical study.

In a topical study, you select and focus on a topic of interest. I believe that this method of study is very beneficial, and it is my personal favourite. In this method of study, we endeavour to get a complete picture of what the Bible teaches about a subject, for example, love.

▶ How are the various methods of Bible study different from one another?

____

____

____

____

____

____

▶ Which one(s) have you practised in the past?

____

____

____

▶ Practically speaking, which method do you find most difficult to implement and why?

____

____

____

____

MEDITATION = HEARING + SPEAKING

> **"***We visualize ourselves in the word and become one with it during meditation, but, we are meditating on who we already are.***"**

Meditation begins when you mutter the verses to yourself. Start your session with prayer and ask the Holy Spirit to give you understanding. Don't try to memorize the verses, just focus on them in your mind as you speak them out. In meditation, you make the verses personal and apply the message in the verses to your life today. See yourself in the verses.

▶ **What does a good actor do before mounting the stage to perform?**

____

____

____

____

▶ **How is acting different from meditation?**

____

____

____

____

▶   What happens as we continue to mutter God's word?

____

____

____

____

____

▶   Is meditation a mind game? Explain your answer.

____

____

____

____

____

The more you meditate the bigger and clearer the picture becomes. You will see yourself differently. The object of meditation is not to finish, the object of meditation is to be changed. You never finish meditating on any verse of scripture because we see from Ephesians 3:10 that the wisdom of God is multifaceted. It is inexhaustible. The more you meditate on a verse the more like Jesus you become.

> **❝** *Christians often dart from church to seminar without feeding on the word they are hearing. They stumble because the word of God isn't rooted in them.* **❞**

According to Romans 10:17, faith comes by hearing and hearing by the word of God. Faith to be and do is not always present. It comes. It is the natural by-product of a process. Paul tells us what that process is—hearing the word of God. How do we hear? We hear when we meditate. When you meditate, you mutter and speak the verse of scripture to yourself. You minister the word of God to your heart by speaking and speaking and speaking God's word to yourself. This produces faith.

►   **Read Joshua 1:8 and Psalm 45:1. Why is speaking crucial to meditation?**

> **"** *During meditation, you minister the word of God to your heart by speaking and speaking and speaking God's word to yourself. This produces faith.* **"**

►   **What is the ultimate goal of meditation?**

Chapter 7

Pure Milk

As newborn babes, desire the pure milk of the word, that you may grow thereby (1 Peter 2:2).

Peter admonishes that we maintain an insatiable desire for God's word in the same way that a baby thirsts for milk. Peter however qualifies what we should thirst for—pure milk.

HEALTHY TEACHING

God reveals His ways and thoughts to us through the word. *Logos,* [5] is the Greek word that is translated as word in Hebrews 4:12. It can be defined as the revealed will of God or the sum of the utterances of God. It is the communication of God to His creation. Before a doctrine is established as the *logos,* before we accept a teaching as an expression of God's revealed will, we must get a balanced view of God's mind about the matter from all His other utterances in scripture on that subject.

---

5   W.E. Vine, *Vine's Expository Dictionary Of New Testament Words* (Virginia: MacDonald Publishing, ISBN 0-917006-03-8), 1252-3.

▶ Read Colossians 2:16-23, Galatians 3, and Hebrews 10:1-4. What were the proponents of Judaism trying to teach the newly converted Christians?

____

____

____

____

▶ Did it differ from what other scriptures taught? If so, how was it different?

____

____

____

____

> **"** *Before we accept a teaching as God's revealed will, we must get a balanced picture of what the whole body of scripture says about the subject.* **"**

The *logos* cannot be obtained from a single verse of scripture taken out of context. Context must be established by understanding the background—to whom was it written and what did it mean to them at that time? Without proper exegesis, we cannot expect to apply the knowledge gained properly.

▶ How can we reduce the risk of misinterpreting scripture?

____

____

____

____

▶ What specific questions can we ask as we examine any doctrine?

____

____

____

____

____

We must take responsibility for what we eat. It shouldn't matter if the person serving the food is the greatest chef in the world, it is our responsibility to ensure that we are not about to be poisoned.

EAT RESPONSIBLY

It is not the intention of most preachers to deceive or knowingly lead people into error. Error could be the result of ignorance on the part of the teacher, or false teaching that they have been subjected to and may not have thoroughly checked out. No teacher is infallible. The only thing we can really count on, is the infallibility of God's word.

▶   How can we guard against exalting the personality teaching the word above the word itself, even if great signs and wonders characterize that person's ministry?

____

____

____

> **"**_No teacher is infallible. The only thing we can count on is the infallibility of God's word._ **"**

▶   If you have been fed false doctrine, who should bear the ultimate responsibility and what can be done about it?

____

____

____

____

____

____

____

Chapter 8

Transformed By The Word

GROWTH BY GRACE NOT SELF-EFFORT

Many of us have missed the whole point of the New Testament, approaching it with an Old Testament mentality. We use the New Testament as a code of law rather than as an enabling tool in our walk of faith. We try to live up to the standard of the law by relying purely on willpower and self-effort instead of the power of God.

The illumination of the Spirit makes alive the truth of scripture. This truth sets the believer free from slavery to the ritual of the law and self-effort in fulfilling it. The way we were saved is the way we grow in Christ and the same way we fulfill His every desire for our lives. If salvation is by grace, then growth in God is by grace, and fulfillment of every requirement of God is by grace. Grace is the power of God available to us to meet our needs and achieve His purpose.

And if by grace, then it is no longer of works; otherwise grace is no longer grace. But if it is of works, it is no longer grace; otherwise work is no longer work (Romans 11:6).

▶ **What does using the New Testament as a code of law look like?**

____

____

____

____

____

"*If salvation is by grace, then growth in God is by grace, and fulfillment of every requirement of God is by grace.***"**

▶ **What role does self-discipline and willpower play in breaking free from harmful habits?**

____

____

____

____

____

2 Corinthians 3:18 summarizes how the New Testament believer grows through the exercise of God's grace.

But we all, with unveiled face, beholding as in a mirror the glory of the Lord, are being transformed into the same image from glory to glory, just as by the Spirit of the Lord.

The Interlinear Greek-English New Testament puts it this way, "But we all having been unveiled..." [6] In the Greek language, every verb is characterized by a tense, mood, and voice. The voice of the phrase, 'having been unveiled', is called the passive voice. The passive voice is used where the subject of the verb is receiving the action. The phrase, 'are transformed', is also in the passive voice. [7] This means that we can't unveil our eyes or change ourselves because the subject of the verb receives the action. The Holy Spirit is the one who unveils our eyes. He is the one who changes us. You cannot change yourself, your habits, or your thinking. So do we just fold our arms, do nothing, and blame the Spirit for not changing us?

The third verb in the verse, 'beholding', is in the middle voice in the Greek. [8] The middle voice is used when the subject of the verb is doing the action for their own benefit. The Spirit of God unveils our eyes and changes us as we behold the Lord.

❝ *Glory beheld, is glory revealed, and glory revealed always leads to transformation.* **❞**

Read the account in Exodus 34:28-29 about how Moses' face was transformed to reflect the glory of God as he beheld the presence of the Lord for forty days. Glory beheld is glory revealed, and glory revealed always produces transformation.

---

6   Rev. Dr. Alfred Marshall, The Interlinear Greek-English New Testament (UK: Samuel Bagster and Sons, 1987), 714.

7   *The Complete Biblical Library New Testament, Romans-Corinthians,* (Missouri: World Library Press, 1991), 532.

8   Ibid., 534.

▶ How does the transformation we desire in our lives occur?

____

____

____

____

▶ Describe how the prescribed New Testament process for transformation differs from what we commonly practice.

____

____

____

____

▶ Why do Christians often not embrace the New Testament way?

____

____

____

____

____

THE SECRET OF TRANSFORMATION

And all of us, as with unveiled face, [because we] continued to behold [in the Word of God] as in a mirror the glory of the Lord, are constantly being transfigured into His very own image in ever increasing splendour and from one degree of glory to another; [for this comes] from the Lord [Who is] the Spirit (2 Corinthians 3:18 AMPCE).

We have misunderstood what it means for the word of God to be called a mirror. A mirror operates by reflecting light from an object into your eyes. When you stand in front of a mirror, it reflects your image back into your eyes so you can see what you look like. People have used the mirror of the word of God as a way of pointing out their flaws. Some ministers have used the mirror of the word of God as a way of getting Christians to see how sinful they are and to get them to change their ways. This is not how the New Testament mirror is to be used. The New Testament mirror is not there to point out your flaws because you cannot change yourself anyway. What we are to look at in this mirror is the radiance and beauty of the Lord in us. When we come to the mirror of the New Testament with an unveiled face, it reflects the radiance of Jesus Christ with all His perfection and beauty. But the mirror also shows us that the radiance is coming out of our hearts.

❝ *The New Testament was not given to show us our flaws, it was given to show us who we are in Christ.* **❞**

▶ Read Ephesians 1:17-23. Why was the New Testament given to us?

____

____

____

The mystery which has been hidden from ages and from generations, but now has been revealed to His saints. To them God willed to make known what are the riches of the glory of this mystery among the Gentiles: which is Christ in you, the hope of glory (Colossians 1:26-27).

The Christ we see in the scriptures is in us. We are new creatures who have the same perfection as Christ. We have the same nature and characteristics as Christ, for the new nature was created after God in righteousness and true holiness (Ephesians 4:24).

The way we behold this glory is through the process of meditation. We keep muttering the truths of who Christ is in us to our hearts and chewing on the truths of who we are in Him. Then the reality of these truths becomes established in our hearts. As we continue to behold this glory of Christ in the word of God, the Spirit of the Lord transforms us into the same image we see.

The word translated 'transformed' in the New Testament, is the Greek word *metamorphoō*, from which we get the English word, metamorphosis.[9] Metamorphosis is the process that a caterpillar undergoes to become a butterfly. If you didn't know better, you would not predict that a caterpillar could become a butterfly. You might not look, sound, or act like a Christian, but the life of Jesus Christ dwells in you once you are born again. As you continue through meditation, to focus on who you are in Christ, your actions will begin to change. Glory beheld is glory revealed, and glory revealed always leads to transformation.

---

9   W.E. Vine, *Vine's Expository Dictionary Of New Testament Words* (Virginia: MacDonald Publishing, ISBN 0-917006-03-8), 1171.

▶ Describe the process of transformation in Christ through meditation in your own words.

____

____

____

____

____

____

____

____

____

Now it was so, when Moses came down from Mount Sinai (and the two tablets of the Testimony were in Moses' hand when he came down from the mountain), that Moses did not know that the skin of his face shone while he talked with Him (Exodus 34:29).

Moses did not know that the skin of his face shone. It was not an instantaneous or dramatic experience. He did not even realize what was happening. We don't always realize what is happening but gradually, our attitudes and our habits change in response to the beholding process. The Christ-life that dwells in your spirit man begins to affect your mind and your body. Your appetites, desires, and priorities change, and you start expressing the glory of Christ from one degree to another.

We can grow in Christ through the operation of His grace and Spirit. This way, just as we can take no credit for our salvation, we can take no credit for our growth and victory in God. All glory belongs to the God of grace. As Paul says in Ephesians 2:7, "In ages to come He might show the exceeding riches of His grace in His kindness towards us in Christ Jesus." David expressed this same powerful secret in Psalm 17 verse 15, "As for me I will behold your face in righteousness. I shall be satisfied when I awake in Your likeness."

▶   We are frequently told to confess the word. How is this type of confession different from meditation?

____

____

____

____

____

____

"*As you continue to behold the glory of the Lord through meditation, your mind and body and your desires and priorities will change.* **"**

▶   How often should we behold the glory of the Lord?

____

____

____

Chapter 9

The Holy Spirit In Meditation

For what man knows the things of a man except the spirit of the man which is in him? Even so no one knows the things of God except the Spirit of God. Now we have received, not the spirit of the world, but the Spirit who is from God, that we might know the things that have been freely given to us by God (1 Corinthians 2:11-12).

THE LORD WHO IS THE SPIRIT

We cannot discover God through scientific investigation or human reasoning. He must reveal Himself to be known. Meditation alone does not give revelation of God to our hearts. The revelation of God comes only from the Spirit. The practice of meditation puts us in a place where the Holy Spirit can give us revelation.

> **"***Meditation puts us in a place where the Holy Spirit can give us revelation.***"**

▶ Read John 14:26, John 15:26, and John 16:13-15. What role does the Holy Spirit play in our lives?

____

____

REVELATION FROM THE SPIRIT

If you walk into a dark room and switch on the light, the light reveals what was always there but hidden because of the darkness. In meditation, we calmly mutter and envision, waiting on the Holy Spirit to bring enlightenment. Meditation is the way we behold the glory of God (2 Corinthians 3:18). However, the Spirit reveals this glory to us and that revelation brings transformation. Our part is to behold and His part is to reveal and transform.

▶   Read Ephesians 1:17-18 and Psalm 119:18. Is meditation a mental exercise where we are trying to figure out who we are in Christ and what we have? Explain your answer.

In meditation, we calmly mutter and envision, waiting on the Holy Spirit to bring enlightenment.

From the Inside Out

We become instantly born again; the Spirit of God recreates us in God's image and takes residence inside us, instantly putting us back in communion with God. This immediate transformation happens in our spirit. However, our soul, which consists of our mind (conscious and subconscious), will, and emotions, remains untouched. The subconscious mind is the seat of our belief systems, limitations, and lusts (evil desires), and largely determines what we do. Any restriction we experience in our lives is a result of limiting belief systems and a clouded understanding of who we are. These belief systems are established as strongholds in our hearts and internal pictures of who we are and what we are capable of.

God remoulds you by replacing the pictures in your heart with new images based on who you are in Christ.

The only way your experience of life will change is if your mind is remoulded in its understanding of who you are in Christ. Until this is done, the internal transformation you have experienced in your spirit remains trapped inside your spirit. The Bible refers to the combination of your subconscious mind and spirit as your heart, the central core of your being. Therefore, what the world around you sees and experiences in their dealings with you, is the worldview that has been established in your heart. This worldview consists of established images that dominate your heart.

▶ Why do our actions not change the instant we become born again?

▶ Examine your worldview, for example your beliefs about romantic love. Can you identify some factors that have contributed to your worldview?

▶ How can our mindsets be changed?

PAINTING IN TECHNICOLOR

> **"** *Revelation is that flash of insight that comes during medita-tion, when the Holy Spirit turns on the light and you see a snapshot of the picture He has painted.* **"**

As you meditate on scripture, your imagination paints a picture of what the verse says about you and the Holy Spirit is actively involved in this process. Imagine the Holy Spirit as a master painter and your heart (your subconscious mind and spirit), as the canvas. The Holy Spirit dips the paintbrush of your imagination into the ink of the word and uses the painting process of meditation to paint a picture of who you are in Christ on the canvas of your heart.

The Holy Spirit uses light we have already received on a verse of scripture, to shed further light on another verse, because one of His roles is to remind us of the things Jesus said. As you meditate on a verse, you often remember another verse that complements it. Get your concordance out to find the verse so you can include it in your meditation.

Revelation is that 'aha' moment, that flash of insight you get during meditation, when you see a snapshot of the picture the Holy Spirit has painted. This snapshot is imprinted in your subconscious mind and replaces any contrary picture that was there before. Once it becomes established in your heart through continued medita-tion, that truth makes you free and the nature of God in your spirit regarding that area finds expression through your transformed soul into your actions.

▶   Have you experienced an 'aha' moment? What were you doing when it occurred?

____

____

____

____

▶   Describe what the Holy Spirit does during meditation in your own words.

____

____

____

____

____

____

▶   How does the picture that the Holy Spirit paints become established in our hearts?

____

____

____

GENERATING THE POWER

You don't need more power. More power than you can ever expend already fills your heart. Once the light of revelation shines into your heart from meditation, the power of God receives expression from your spirit into that area you are meditating on and dispels darkness, fear, and limitation, and you instantly experience the freedom of a transformed life.

Meditation is a deeply spiritual process that gets the word to its destination, which is the spiritual man. As you meditate, the word nourishes your spirit because your spirit consumes the word in the same way that you consume food. The word also changes the belief systems of your subconscious mind. Once the belief systems are changed internally, your conscious mind is informed of who you are. Since the new information is coming from a foundation of God's word and from the depth of your heart, the conscious mind does not challenge it. Your conscious mind is the last beneficiary of the process. There is plenty happening that you are not aware of. You are changing from the inside out.

Meditation is a deeply spiritual process that gets the word to its destination, which is the spiritual man. Your conscious mind is the last beneficiary of this process.

▶ Have you ever tried to lose weight through diet and exercise or do you know anyone who has? Did you or did they see appreciable results immediately? Describe what happened.

▶   Why is it important not to get discouraged if you are meditating on scripture and have not yet seen change?

____

____

____

____

____

____

____

____

Chapter 10

Atmosphere of Meditation

We can make our times of meditation more effective by recognising that there is a certain heart atmosphere necessary to help us connect to the operation of the Holy Spirit. The Holy Spirit operates everywhere and is not intimidated by noise, chaos or even sin. However for the seeker, we can easily miss His operations in our lives and it is therefore us for whom preparation is necessary.

Like Prophet Habakkuk in Habakkuk 2:1-2, we can take a posture that would enable us to better perceive His leading. Habakkuk resolves to place himself on his observatory and look out for revelation, which the Lord would give in answer to his questions. This was a place where he could be far away from the noise and bustle of men and there turn his eyes towards heaven and direct his collected mind towards God, to look out for a revelation. [10] Whether this was an actual place he went to or not, we know he recognised the need for quiet.

The greatest challenge to spiritual growth in the modern era is not sin. It is distraction.

---

10   Keil & Delitzsch, *Commentary on the Old Testament, Minor Prophets, Volume 10* (Massachusetts: Hendrickson Publishers, Inc 2001),399.

▶   What are the primary causes of distraction you experience during your times of meditation? How have you overcome them?

> *" The Lord will typically not shout above the noise to be heard, He would rather wait on us to want Him enough to quieten down to listen to His still small voice. "*

▶   Read Genesis 24:63. Where is your own quiet place which you find most effective for meditation?

David the King had a similar practice:

I will bless the LORD who has given me counsel; My heart also instructs me in the night seasons. (Psalm 16:7).

When I remember You on my bed, I meditate on You in the night watches (Psalm 63:6).

▶ Read Job 33:14-16 and Mark 13:35. Do you believe the night watches are a time of strong visitation? Give reasons for your answer.

____

____

____

____

▶ Discuss your use of worship, music and speaking in tongues in quietening your heart. Which have you found most effective?

____

____

____

THE QUIET HEART

Therefore lay aside all filthiness and overflow of wickedness, and receive with meekness the implanted word, which is able to save your souls (James 1:21)

So get rid of all the filth and evil in your lives, and humbly accept the word God has planted in your hearts, for it has the power to save your souls (James 1:21 NLT)

The word 'meek' is translated from the Greek word *praótes* which according to Vines, is 'that temper of spirit in which we accept His dealings with us as good, and therefore without disputing or resisting'[11]. A meek heart is one which approaches the Lord with a readiness to obey, willingness to be corrected and openness to change.

▶   **Read Psalm 131. How can one develop a meek heart?**

---

11   *W. E. Vine, A Comprehensive Dictionary of the Original Greek Words with their Precise Meanings for English Readers* (Virginia: MacDonald Publishing Company ISBN 0-917006-03-8), 736

Part Three
The Life of Meditation

Chapter 11

Maintaining A Balanced Diet

WHAT YOU EAT IS WHAT YOU GET

You are what you eat. You can eat a full meal every day, but if it is not a balanced meal, there will be a deficiency in your life which will be evident to all. When I went on the Atkins diet for two weeks and ate only proteins, I had a drastic reduction in energy, which adversely affected my productivity. It doesn't matter whether or not you count calories; your body counts every calorie you consume and banks every single one. If your diet is high in carbohydrates and fat, that fact will be there for all to see.

The same principle applies in our spiritual lives. Progress will only be made in the areas where you spend time in meditation. When you meditate on God's word in a particular area, faith energy is produced, empowering you to walk in love, joy, prosperity, peace, and to carry out the things God expects you to do.

Meditate on these things; give yourself entirely to them, that your progress may be evident to all (1 Timothy 4:15).

Progress is continuous advancement in the direction of your goal. Focus on what God's word says about you and let that be what you say about yourself and what you choose to believe, irrespective of external circumstances. As you maintain your consistency, the strength of God will begin to fill your heart and your progress will be evident to all.

▶ Name two factors that enable us make progress in our spiritual lives and beyond.

____

____

> **“**_Progress is only made in areas where you meditate. You will experience weakness and susceptibility to temptation in areas where you spend no time meditating._**”**

OVERCOMING WEAKNESS

If there is an area of your life where you are having difficulty living correctly or walking in what you know to be God's will, you shouldn't be alarmed neither should you bury your head in the sand. All that your weakness demonstrates is a deficiency in your diet. If you had an iron deficiency, to remedy the situation you wouldn't start increasing your vitamin C intake would you? No, you would increase your intake of iron-rich foods or take iron supplements. Spiritually, all you would need to do is double up on your meditation on God's word in that area.

> **“**_Focus on the solution, not the problem. Feed on the solution and that is who you become as you meditate._**”**

It surprises me that people who are facing problems in a certain area, only read a general daily devotional study guide for their daily Bible study. Progress is only evident in the areas of your life where you spend time in meditation. Look for verses of scripture, which address the issue that you are having difficulties with. By that, I don't mean find scriptures that command you not to commit that act. Find verses that talk about the power available to overcome that sin.

For example, if you are dealing with anger, focusing on Galatians 5:20, which identifies outbursts of wrath as one of the works of the flesh will not help. You will be better off meditating on Romans 6:6, "knowing this, that our old man was crucified with Him that the body of sin might be done away with, that we should no longer serve sin." Feed on the solution not the problem.

▶ **What should you do about areas of your life where you are weak and vulnerable to Satan's attacks?**

____

____

____

____

▶ **If you fall back into old patterns of behaviour, what should you do?**

____

____

____

____

▶ **When and how will your transformation occur?**

____

____

____

> *Trying to walk in the power of God's word without developing a habit of meditation is like trying to lift a heavy weight without having eaten for a month.*

Shock waves go through the local, national, or international Christian community when a popular Christian minister falls into sexual sin or financial impropriety, or is consumed by pride. The fearful thought that crosses peoples' minds is, if that can happen to him, what hope is there for me?

Christian ministers are particularly prone to an unhealthy spiritual diet. Serving people and teaching people God's word creates the illusion to ministers and those observing them, that they are spiritually strong. It is possible for a baker whose bakery is the talk of the community to die of starvation if he does not consume what he bakes.

SUSTAINABLE ENERGY

> *But those who wait on the Lord*
> *Shall renew their strength;*
> *They shall mount up with wings like eagles,*
> *They shall run and not be weary,*
> *They shall walk and not faint (Isaiah 40:31).*

The word 'wait' in this passage is the Hebrew word *qâvâh*, which according to Strong's Exhaustive Concordance, means to bind together by twisting. [12] The image

---

12   James H. Strong, *Strong's Exhaustive Concordance* (Michigan: Baker Book House, 1989), H6960

here is that of strengthening a weak rope by putting it in a weave with stronger ropes. When we wait on God through meditation, we are weaving ourselves to Him. The more we meditate, the more we weave ourselves to Him, and our strength is renewed. Through this process, we exchange our weakness for His strength.

▶   Read Isaiah 40:30. Is it possible to live victoriously, in any area of our lives in our own strength? Why?

Spiritual development comes through the application of spiritual energy. No spiritual energy, no spiritual advancement. It's important to maintain a balanced diet, so study a variety of subjects that will help you to develop a healthy Christian lifestyle, starting with the greatest areas of need in your life.

YOU'VE GOT THE POWER

I say then: Walk in the Spirit, and you shall not fulfill the lust of the flesh (Galatians 5:16).

Typically, this verse is read this way, don't walk in the flesh and you will be considered spiritual by God. So we familiarize ourselves with those things that God tells us not to do and try hard not to do them. But that was never how God ordained for us to walk in victory over sin. Here's the correct application of the verse: if you focus on who God says you are and meditate on that, you will keep advancing in your Christian walk. Your unsavoury habits will increasingly drop from your life because of the progress you will be making in the things of God. You wouldn't even realize how drastically your life is changing.

▶ What should a spiritual balanced diet look like?

____

____

____

____

____

▶ Read Matthew 11:30. If Jesus is to be believed, and He is, why is the Christian life a struggle to some?

____

____

____

____

____

____

▶ How can we achieve practical victory over sin?

____

____

____

> *If you meditate on who God says you are, you will keep advancing in your Christian walk and your unsavoury habits will increasingly drop from your life.*

The results of your diet will always become evident. It is never immediate but ultimately, the results of your diet will be evident to all. Where your diet is deficient, your weakness will be evident, and where your diet is sufficient, your strength will ultimately be evident.

Chapter 12

A Prosperous Journey

NO WAY OUT?

It is almost amusing thinking about it now, but for many years I got myself into all sorts of trouble because I misunderstood the following verse of scripture in 1 Corinthians 10:13.

> *No temptation has overtaken you except such as is common to man; but God is faithful, who will not allow you to be tempted beyond what you are able, but with the temptation will also make the way of escape, that you may be able to bear it.*

I interpreted this verse to mean that Satan needed to seek God's permission before he could tempt me. God would allow the temptation if He thought I could handle it. I imagined that God would create some sort of escape route, a supernatural hatch in the heavens to prevent me from giving in. What I couldn't figure out was why I kept falling flat on my face when temptation came my way, and why the way out never seemed to materialize.

> **"***If God's word is not hidden in your heart through meditation, the doorway of escape will remain shut.***"**

THE WAY OF ESCAPE

The light of God's word finally shone through my ignorance when I discovered 2 Peter 1:2-4.

Grace and peace be multiplied to you in the knowledge of God and of Jesus our Lord, as His divine power has given to us all things that pertain to life and godliness, through the knowledge of Him who called us by glory and virtue, by which have been given to us exceedingly great and precious promises, that through these you may be partakers of the divine nature, having escaped the corruption that is in the world through lust.

► **Read Psalm 119:11. How can we find the way of escape in every temptation?**

____

____

____

____

____

The outcome of our lives is not purely the result of divine action. Crying out to God to come through for us is not the recipe for success that God recommended to Joshua.

*This Book of the Law shall not depart from your mouth, but you shall medi-
itate in it day and night, that you may observe to do according to all that
is written in it. For then you will make your way prosperous, and then you
will have good success (Joshua 1:8).*

There is a God-ward side and a man-ward side in the equation of life. God
provides the power and man, by faith, uses what God has provided to experience
the results God intends.

▶ **Why is 'crying out to God for a breakthrough' not recommended?**

PROSPERITY GOD'S STYLE

The word 'prosperous' in Joshua 1:8, is rendered in the Septuagint (the Greek
translation of the Old Testament), as the verb, *euodoomai*. It literally means to be
led along a good road or to have a good journey. [13] So, God wants us to have a good
journey through life.

---

13   *The Complete Biblical Library Greek-English Dictionary Delta-Epsilon*, (Missouri: World Library Press, 1990), 642.

▶ **What is your idea of a good journey?**

____

____

____

____

____

Prosperity, God's style, is a total state of well-being: spiritually, mentally, physically, financially and socially. His desire is that we abide in a state of an overflow of divine energy in every aspect of our lives and relationships. God guarantees that when we meditate on His word and obey His counsel, we will deal wisely in all the affairs of life and have a good journey through life.

▶ **What is man's side of the prosperity equation?**

____

____

____

____

____

❝ *Crying out to God to come through for us is not the recipe for success that God recommended to Joshua.* **❞**

LIVING FOR A BREAKTHROUGH

God's will for our lives is not to live from one miracle to the next. A miracle is a suspension of the normal course of things. It is an intervention by the power of God to rectify something out of order. God created the earth through the exercise of a miracle. Genesis 1:2 paints a picture of a chaotic situation on earth, which took a miracle to restore. God created life with the ability to propagate itself so that He would not need to speak every subsequent new life into being. God does not reach into the earth anymore to form the body of a human being as He did with Adam and Eve. After He created them, He blessed them and told them to be fruitful and multiply (Genesis 1:28).

Thus, we see that God didn't intend for us to live hopping from one breakthrough to another. Although God still performs miracles today, miracles are a correction of things or situations that have gone out of line with the order God ordained in the beginning. Adam and Eve did not need miracles in the Garden of Eden.

WHAT DID JESUS DO?

When Jesus was on earth, He showed us what God is like (John 1:18). Jesus performed miracles to fix the lives of others that were broken. However, we rarely see Him performing a miracle for Himself. We don't see Him crying out to God for a breakthrough for Himself. The enemy persecuted Him, but we don't see Him in disarray, perturbed, seeking God to come through for Him. He always operated on an even keel.

▶ **Read John 14:12. How does God intend for us to live?**

____

____

____

▶ How can we live life without peaks and troughs, without needing a miracle at every corner?

____

____

____

____

____

____

LIFE ON AN EVEN KEEL

> *But his delight is in the law of the Lord,*
> *And in His law he meditates day and night.*
> *He shall be like a tree*
> *Planted by the rivers of water,*
> *That brings forth its fruit in its season,*
> *Whose leaf also shall not wither; (Psalm 1:2-3).*

A tree planted by the rivers of water, paints a picture of stability and peace. It denotes somebody who, through meditation, has located himself in a place of continuous supply of nutrients and stability. It is not a picture of someone running from miracle to miracle or darting from place to place trying to make things work.

God doesn't determine where our tree is positioned. We do by the choice we make to meditate or not, on His word. The Bible goes on to say that his leaf also shall not wither, which indicates constant productivity. In other words, he will have a good journey. This is God's recipe for living for you.

> **"** *God guarantees that if we meditate on His word and obey His counsel, we will deal wisely in all the affairs of life and have a good journey through life.* **"**

▶ Given what you have learnt, what can you do to make your life prosperous or more prosperous than it currently is?

____

____

____

____

____

____

▶ We are what we repeatedly do. How are you going to implement your strategies practically?

____

____

____

____

____

Appendices

Inspired Prayers

These prayers have been compiled primarily from the inspired prayers of the Apostle Paul for the New Testament churches. Meditate on and pray portions of these daily.

Father, I pray that You, the God of my Lord Jesus Christ, the glorious Father, may give me the spirit of wisdom and revelation, so that I may know You better.

I pray that the eyes of my heart may be enlightened, in order that I may know the hope to which You have called me, (to know) the riches of your glorious inheritance in the saints, and (to know) your incomparably great power for us who believe. That power, which is like the working of your mighty strength, which You exerted in Christ when You raised Him from the dead and seated Him at your right hand in the heavenly realms, far above all rule and authority, power and dominion, and every title that can be given, not only in the present age but also in the one to come.

I pray that out of your glorious riches, You may strengthen me with power through your Spirit in my inner being, so that Christ may dwell in my heart through faith; that I being rooted and established in love, may have power, together with all the saints, to grasp how wide and long and high and deep is the love of Christ, and to know this love that surpasses knowledge (in order) that I may be filled to the measure of all the fullness of God.

I pray that my love may abound more and more in knowledge and depth of insight, so that I may be able to discern what is best, and may be pure and blameless until the day of Christ, filled with the fruit of righteousness that comes through Jesus Christ, to the glory and praise of God.

I ask that You fill me with the knowledge of your will through all spiritual wisdom and understanding; that I may live a life worthy of the Lord and may please You in every way [by] bearing fruit in every good work [and] growing in the knowledge of God, being strengthened with all power according to your glorious might so that I may have great endurance and patience and joyfully giving thanks to You Father, who has qualified me to share in the inheritance of the saints in the kingdom of light.

Jesus, I long to progressively become more deeply and intimately acquainted with You, perceiving and recognizing and understanding the wonders of your person more strongly and clearly, and that I may in the same way come to know the power outflowing from your resurrection, that I may so share your sufferings so as to be continually transformed in spirit into your likeness even to your death, in the hope that if possible I may attain to the spiritual and moral resurrection that lifts me out from among the dead even while in the body.

Father, I thank You for blessing me with all spiritual blessings in heavenly places in Christ. I pray that You enlarge my spiritual capacity to dream bigger dreams, my mental capacity to walk in your wisdom, my social influence to impact more people for your kingdom and my financial capacity to give generously to every good work. Let your hand on me be strong and keep me from harm.

Jesus, judge me severely daily, correct me ruthlessly so that I may serve You more perfectly. Show me the level of my present deception regarding what I know that I may continually lose confidence in myself and place my confidence in You more and more. Above all, I ask for your grace in my daily walk with You, that I may do your will all the days of my life. In Jesus name.

Essential Study Helps

a. Online Resources

To say that my list of recommended online resources is not exhaustive is a major understatement. The resources I use may not even be the best out there but they are the ones that I have come across and found beneficial. Try them out but also carry out your own search and let me know what you find (you can reach me at carlton-williams.com).

Two sites I find useful and visit often for online translations and commentaries are biblehub.com and biblegateway.com.

Many apps are available and a simple Google search will turn up numerous applications you can try out. Sometimes it is just about finding one that fits your style and way of working. I like the New Spirit Filled Bible app. Having used and loved the hardcopy version for many years, I jumped at the app as soon as I knew it was available.

The Greek Interlinear Bible from PhotoKandy Studios and CWP-Teacher from CWP software, both on the Apple App Store, are my go-to interlinear Bibles.

When I discovered that LifeWay had made available its 39-Volume Complete Biblical Library (CBL), Old and New Testament as an app, I jumped at it. It is complete with Old and New Testament Study Bibles, a Hebrew-English Dictionary, a Greek-English Dictionary, a Various Versions volume, a Harmony of the Gospels, and a Greek Grammar. Old and New Testament sets can be purchased separately. Check out wordsearchbible.com and do a search on CBL.

b. Essential Study Bibles

As a serious Bible student, there are certain Bible translations you've got to have. I'll list them in order of priority.

1. A good Study Bible: a good study Bible will provide a good cross-reference, commentary, useful maps, and concordance. The New Spirit Filled Bible published by Thomas Nelson, which integrates its pentecostal-charismatic viewpoint is my personal favourite.

2. An Amplified Bible: for the sake of brevity in translation, certain nuances conveyed in the original language or word construction have to be omitted in a regular translation. Where several words in the English language would be required to better express the shades of meaning expressed in the original Hebrew or Greek text, a regular translation would select the best single word our limited English language has to offer. The Amplified Bible does not impose this restriction on itself. It should not be your only study Bible because you might find it a bit tedious at times, but oh the richness!

3. The Word, The Bible from 26 Translations: this covers both the Old and New Testaments. It renders each verse in the King James Version, but also lets you know where it is rendered differently from a source of 26 different translations.

4. The Message Bible: Eugene Peterson's The Message Bible, is a Bible in contemporary language. It uses contemporary slang from the US rather than more neutral International English but this keeps the language current, fresh, and understandable, as it says in its introduction, and I agree.

c. *Study Aids in Print*

Here is the original study helps list I received when I attended Grace Bible School in Tulsa. I still find these study aids invaluable today. I've left my Dean, Geof Jackson's original comments (printed by permission). Be sure to keep number nine secret.

1. Strong's Exhaustive Concordance of the Bible - James Strong

Many publishers; make sure you purchase one with the Hebrew and Greek dictionaries.

2. The Interlinear Greek-English New Testament (Baker) - Jay P. Green, Sr.

This edition is especially useful for the English reading student since it also has the Strong's word numbers above each Greek word. Other editions of this resource are also available but do not have Strong's word numbers.

3. The Englishman's Greek Concordance of the New Testament (Hendrickson) - George V. Wigram

Essential tool for study of New Testament word use. This edition is keyed to the Strong's number system.

4. The Vine's Complete Expository Dictionary of Old and New Testament Words (Nelson) - W.E. Vine

There are other publishers, but this one is keyed to the Strong's number system for easy cross reference. This is an extremely useful and easy-to-use study book.

5. The Linguistic Key to the Greek New Testament (Zondervan) - Fritz Rienecker and Cleon Rogers

My favourite tool. This little volume is the single most useful book I have found. It requires some working knowledge of Greek (no more than familiarity with what we have studied), and an interlinear New Testament.

6. Trench's Synonyms of the New Testament (Baker Book House) - R.C. Trench

This edition is nicely reprinted and coded to the Strong's number system. It is the standard work on Greek synonyms.

7. Word Studies in the Greek New Testament 4 Volumes (Eerdmans) - Kenneth Wuest

The best and easiest to use of the New Testament Word Studies available. It covers most of the New Testament, offering tremendous insights and help into the Greek treasures. Volumes 1 and 2 are scriptural commentary, volume 3 is a topical and word study collection, and volume 4 is an expanded translation of the New Testament.

8. Vincent's Word Studies of the New Testament, 4 volumes (Hendrickson) - Marvin R. Vincent

Complete word studies of the New Testament. It is not as detailed as Wuest, but a valuable resource to have.

9. New Testament Words (Westminster Press) - William Barclay

A tremendous resource for the history and use of nearly 70 significant Greek words and their derivatives. One of these insights can illuminate your study and message beyond your fondest dreams. (Don't tell people about this book, they'll think you are a genius).

10. The IVP Bible Background Commentary: Old Testament - Walton Matthews and Chavalas

An indispensable resource for all students of the Bible, accessibly providing the cultural background of every passage in the Old Testament.

11. The IVP Bible Background Commentary: New Testament - Keener

An indispensable resource for all students of the Bible, accessibly providing the cultural background of every passage in the New Testament.

12. The Complete Word Study New Testament (amg pub.) - Spiros Zodhiates

This study tool contains the KJV text with interlinear notation of both the Strong's number and a grammatical notations code for every word. Strong's Greek dictionary is found in the back of the volume along with:

a)   an excellent comparative dictionary written by the author

b)   a key to the analysis code for grammatical notations

c)   an abbreviated Greek concordance

This is an excellent and very usable addition to your library.

13. The Complete Word Study Dictionary, New Testament (amg) - Spiros Zodhiates

Designed to be used in conjunction with the above, this is a very complete dictionary. It is based on the Greek words, numbered to Strong's, and offers more in-depth information: word origin, textual usage, and synonym comparison than the above volume as well as some other tools.

14. The Complete Biblical Library: New Testament, 17 Volumes (World Library

Press)

As the title reflects, this is a complete system of word study and commentary. The set contains 9 volumes of the most well-designed interlinear New Testament available, complete with verse by verse commentary, and alternate translations. There are 6 volumes of the most detailed and easy-to-use Greek dictionaries, linked to the Interlinear Bible by an excellent numbering system. The 16th volume is a very useful Harmony of the Gospels and the 17th volume is the best Greek Grammar review I have ever seen. An excellent set of tools that will replace many of the other reference works and offer some help that no other set does.

Bibliography

1. Jamieson Robert, Fausset A.R., and Brown David. *A Commentary On The Old And New Testament, Volume 2.* Massachusetts: Hendrickson, 1997.

2. Marshall A. Rev. Dr. *The Interlinear Greek-English New Testament.* UK: Samuel Bagster and Sons, 1987.

3. Strong James H. *Strong's Exhaustive Concordance.* Michigan: Baker Book House, 1989.

4. *The Complete Biblical Library New Testament, Romans - Corinthians.* Missouri: World Library Press, 1991.

5. *The Complete Biblical Library Greek-English Dictionary Delta-Epsilon.* Missouri: World Library Press, 1990.

6. *The Complete Biblical Library Greek-English Dictionary Lamda-Omicron.* Missouri: World Library Press, 1990.

7. Vine W.E. *Vine's Expository Dictionary Of New Testament Words.* Virginia: MacDonald Publishing, ISBN 0-917006-03-8.

8. Keil & Delitzsch. *Commentary on the Old Testament, Minor Prophets, Volume 10.* Massachusetts: Hendrickson Publishers, Inc 2001.

About the Author

Carlton Babatunde Williams

Carlton's life mission is to help people discover and demonstrate their God-given purpose, leading to the joy of personal fulfilment and service to humanity.

He has a clear and passionate teaching style, helping believers to see who they are in Christ so that they may live lives of impact and relevance to God's glory. Whether speaking to thousands at international teaching conferences or smaller groups at local assemblies, Carlton's belief that one person can make a difference to a generation is expressed in his passion and focus on the individual.

His ministry roots started in 1985 during his college days where he pioneered a Christian fellowship called The Love Ward. This fellowship grew to several hundred strong and served as the foundation for many Christian ministers who are in active ministry today.

After his ordination in 2001 under Grace Fellowship in Tulsa, he founded The Wordcentre: a vibrant and dynamic church in the heart of London, teaching God's word with a refreshing approach. He also founded and was dean of INSIGHT, a weekend Bible training programme focused on establishing the believer in practical application of doctrinal truth.

Carlton moved to Nigeria in 2007 where he established High Life Church and is expanding into different ministries all armed with the purpose of helping people explore, experience, express, and exhibit the higher life of God with joy.

He completed his doctoral studies with the North Carolina College of Theology in 2017 where he obtained a Th.D. His quest for continuous learning has made him a voracious reader.

He loves to cycle, play chess, and listen to music.

He lives with his wife Anita and has four children: Vanessa, Keona, Zain, and Zoella.

Other Books by Carlton Babatunde Williams

Biblical Meditation: The Secret to a Transformed Life

This book dispels the myths surrounding meditation and provides a comprehensive look at the role of meditation in unlocking the transforming power of God in the life of the Christian. It also offers step-by-step guidance into this practice that has the potential to ignite revival fire in every heart.

Chew on This

Dynamic short teachings that cover a wide range of topics for Christian living such as, The Sent Ones and Prepare For Increase, that will fill your times of meditation with joy.

For more information about Carlton Williams, outreaches and ministry, and our media and other materials, please visit:

Website: *www.carltonwilliams.com*
Facebook: *www.facebook.com/carlton.williams1*
Twitter: *www.twitter.com/pastorcarlton*

Contact Carlton Williams:
info@carltonwilliams.com

9 780995 704312